Zen Life Balance

BECOME THE MASTER OF
YOUR EMOTIONAL THERMOSTAT

- A journey of being increasingly mindful in every area of your life to allow a state of satisfaction and a sense of peace to exist in the mind, body, and soul, as well as *all* aspects of life.

- Elevate feelings of well-being through increased conscious connection with your divine self.

- Quiet the mind and choose to focus on thoughts that feel good. Ease anxiety, stress, and overthinking to allow what you want to flow into your life.

**Darkness Cannot Survive
When Light Is Present**

DARLENE ALISA

BALBOA.PRESS
A DIVISION OF HAY HOUSE

Balboa Press books may be ordered through booksellers or by contacting:

Balboa Press
A Division of Hay House
1663 Liberty Drive
Bloomington, IN 47403
www.balboapress.com
844-682-1282

Print information available on the last page.

ISBN: 979-8-7652-2573-8 (sc)
ISBN: 979-8-7652-2574-5 (e)

Library of Congress Control Number: 2022903889

Balboa Press rev. date: 03/16/2022

This book is dedicated to all the beautiful souls who have a desire to feel a greater sense of peace, satisfaction, and contentment in this current moment, regardless of what anyone thinks, says, or does.

Nothing can hold you back.

Nothing.

The goal is to feel a sense of internal peace wherever one is in life, regardless of the conditions or what anybody else thinks, says, or does.

We are taught at a very young age that conditions in life are the deciding factor to how we should feel—satisfied or unsatisfied, happy or sad, at peace or angry. We are conditioned to meet the expectations of others and ourselves for how things should be or what we should do, think, and feel. When others are happy with us or do things that are pleasing, our emotional thermostat goes up. We feel good. When life doesn't go according to our expectations or someone is displeased with us, our emotional thermostat goes down, possibly along with our self-worth.

Over time we can lose our sense of self: who we are and what makes us happy. We begin to allow external factors to adjust our emotional thermostat up and down. We may feel unable to control our emotions or even want to give up altogether.

Zen Life Balance is about giving yourself the permission to feel as good as you are able to in the current moment, not waiting for others or outside conditions to change and adjust your emotional thermostat for you. It is about looking for even the smallest reason to feel good, everywhere you go, no matter where you're at in life.

Consistent practice will allow you to become the master of your emotional thermostat and empower you to choose how you want to feel at any given time. And when you choose to feel good, everything else will start to fall into place.

Become the Master of Your Emotional Thermostat

"Control over the way you feel, over your response to things, over your response to others, or your response to situations is not only the key to your consistent happiness, but to everything you desire as well."

—Abraham Hicks

"The very moment the thought you choose to focus on feels uncomfortable, LET IT GO and choose a better feeling one."

—Darlene Alisa

"If you are distressed by anything external, the pain is not due to the thing itself but to your estimate of it, and this you have the power to revoke at any moment."

—Marcus Arelius, second-century Roman emperor

Welcome to *Zen Life Balance*!

When you are the master of your emotional thermostat (your thoughts, emotions, attitude/mood, words, actions, and deciding how you want to feel in any given moment) you will experience:

Internal and external peace, serenity, inspiration, love, a sense of well-being, feeling better, patience, happiness, and alignment

When you allow conditions and others to control your emotional thermostat and are living on the surface, life will feel like a struggle.

You may feel stressed and out of sync, have anxiety, irritability, poor health, worry, anger, guilt, depression, fear, a tendency to judge and find fault with self and others while experiencing misalignment.

Directions for practicing the *Zen Life Balance* tools:

This book is meant to be a daily workbook and journal. Carry it everywhere with you to keep you inspired. There is no particular order in which you need to follow all the tools as they will resonate with each person on different levels at different times. As you look through the book, find the tool that resonates with you the most and start there. The left side of the page is to give you inspiration. The right side is for you to write down your desires connected to the *Zen Life Balance* tool and to make notes of inspiration, observations (of self and others), relative quotes and aha moments. Spend a day or two or three or more working with the chosen tool, practicing it every day or looking for examples in life that reflect the tool as you learn to practice it. Start each day with unwavering intention to connect with the *Zen Life Balance* tool throughout the day.

The goal is to become consistent at practicing all the tools every day for the rest of your life. This is what creates an amazing life! Try it.

Self

Living a Zen life begins within. It is about reawakening our conscious connection to our divine inner self (mind, body, and soul)—what we think, experience, and feel. And when our individual well-being of our mind, body and soul is being tended to in a conscious manner, that energy is what we get in return. The environment we live in, what we experience in life and our health are simply a match to our thoughts, feelings, and emotions.

Sometimes we become so focused on misaligned thoughts, feelings, and emotions for so long that we can only look outward for the quality of our lives, often blaming others for the way we feel or the habits we've created that don't serve us for the greater good. **We need to return to our *self* and take accountability for the thoughts we put focus on**. If we give our attention to our feelings, emotions, conversations, and actions throughout each day, we will create better quality health, happiness, love, and a life worth embracing every day—and so much more!

Then we realize the power we have had all along. When you find yourself feeling anything but a sense of peace and happiness, it is time to align yourself with the *Zen Life Balance* tools. **It is about progressing yourself forward from wherever you currently are, one step at a time, to living your best life imaginable; this will radiate out to others around you.**

Believe that anything is possible

Connect with your divine self

Inspire yourself and others

Be mindful of your thoughts.
They become your words
Be mindful of your words.
They become your actions
Be mindful of your actions.
They become your habits
Be mindful of your habits.
They become your character
Be mindful of your character.
It becomes your destiny
Change your thoughts.
Change your destiny.

"Mindful living is a lifestyle. It's a way of consciously walking a sacred earth experience, incorporating purpose and an awareness of Divine Presence in all that we say, think and do on our journey in this lifetime. Discovering the authentic Self will never have a point of arrival because the Self we seek is Infinite."

—Dennis Merrit Jones, *The Art of Uncertainty*

"The secret of change is to focus all of your energy, not on fighting the old, but on building the new."

—Socrates

•Love•

The key that opens the heart and radiates out to the world

•Hope•

The dream that awakens the soul

•Peace•

The light that guides the way

•Faith•

The certainty that sees us through

"Internal and External Peace

begin with the ability to

step back,

quiet the mind

and see everything

and everyone

clearly and without judgement

(through the eyes of love)."

—Darlene Alisa

No matter where we've come from,

we must let go of our past,

learn to be fully present in the current moment and

allow our dreams to come to fruition.

By believing that we are worthy of receiving

anything we desire,

no matter how small or grand it may be,

we empower our inner strength

to achieve our desired greatness

and in turn inspire others.

Quiet the Mind

Live Mindfully

Walk in Faith

Be in Peace …

Zen Life Balance

Contents

Introduction

The only things we have control of in life are: our perception of what happens, which thoughts we choose to focus on and how we choose to respond to the events in our lives. Let go of the feeling that you need to control things or be responsible for everything and everyone, and watch the chaos and drama disappear. Your health gets better, aches and pains of the body decrease, and the physical and emotional stress weighing you down will begin to lift. Pay attention to what you're focusing on and adjust accordingly to allow the happenings in your life to change for the better.

Choose to see the beauty in everything, and your response to what appears stressful will allow peace to lead the way. Life is not just randomly happening to you; it's happening because of what you're focusing on and how you are choosing to see it and allow it to affect you. Leave the past in the past (including five minutes ago). Take responsibility for where you're at in life instead of pointing fingers, blaming others, and being the victim. It's OK that others believe differently than you. *Discover and live your own truth and let others do the same.*

Every moment is a new opportunity to live more happily—relaxed and at peace. Become curious about things you don't understand. Why do you believe what you believe? Does that way of thinking serve you? Release the need to categorize and label everything. Life is always evolving, so the labels we place on something or someone can change in a moment, which means we must continue to evolve the way we see things, as they are forever changing. When we allow ourselves to be fluid and flexible, we can navigate life with ease instead of breaking from being too rigid in our thoughts and actions.

Seasoned surfers are patient in waiting for the right moment to make a move; they study the wave that's heading their way and are aware of and focused on their surroundings. The only thing they know is that the wave is taking them closer to shore, and they must stay flexible and adjust to every movement of the graceful yet powerful wave. They have no control over the actual wave. The only control they have is whether they lean into it and allow the journey to take place or stay rigid and fight the wave, ultimately ending in a complete loss of freedom followed by the pain of the crash.

✸✸✸

Be present.

Find your balance.

Lean into it.

Live Zen.

✸✸✸

The journey of life can—and most likely will—be full of obstacles, hurdles, and sometimes mountains. All of these will involve some aspect of physical, mental, and emotional response, both from within and from others. The goal is to learn more about ourselves and others when these roadblocks appear; then we can move forward in our personal growth and continue to progress toward our desires in life instead of repeating old patterns and situations that lead back to the same outcomes and frustrations.

If we are living a conscious, mindful, balanced life and have an idea of where we are headed, roadblocks (a.k.a. stressful situations) can become visible and navigated with ease, sometimes even avoided.

An *obstacle* is something that slows us down or trips us up along the way, but with the right focus and determination, we quickly get back on our feet and keep going. Pay attention to your surroundings and with whom you surround yourself.

A *hurdle* is something we have to get over, whether we jump, climb, or get support from others to help pull or push us over. Be conscious of whether those around you are helping or holding you back from achieving the mental, emotional, and physical well-being you desire. Well-intentioned people in our lives are coming from their own mental, emotional, and physical places and own belief systems. They may unknowingly pass along their fears, negativity, and imbalances instead of lending positive and balanced support.

A *mountain* is something that, at first glance, may seem impossible to get past, and that—no matter what—getting to the other side is not something we can imagine ever happening. We allow what seem to be our mental, physical, and emotional limitations to hinder us from achievement. Our friends and family will support our hesitations and perceived limitations, particularly if they feel hesitant about the possibility of getting to the other side of the mountain themselves. If you hold positivity and believe there is a way, although you may not know how it can or will happen, and you consistently hold that vision, then it will indeed happen. *Let go of how things have to happen, in which order and at what pace.* Our goal in life is to hold the vision of what we would like to experience and continue to believe that it is, in fact, possible regardless of what anybody else says or thinks or even based on past and current events. Action is still required in the process though. We cannot just sit still and expect things to happen. *We must chose to focus on good-feeling thoughts.*

We are the ones who write our story. What story have you been talking about when it comes to your everyday life?

When dealing with issues, struggles, and frustrations when others are involved, keep in mind that they are coming from their own belief systems. So even though they may be extremely well-intentioned, learn to trust your intuition— that inner feeling, the still small voice within that will guide you through the toughest moments in life when those around you are coming from a place of fear, doubt or imbalance. *Quiet the mind and allow your internal guidance system to come into play and guide you, via your personal path of least resistance, to wherever you desire to go.*

It is the still, small voice within that holds all the answers we can access when we breathe, quiet our minds, and live mindfully and in balance.

Zen Life Balance.

It is good to account for our personal strengths and the strengths of those around us and to take account of our weaknesses, as well as taking (quiet) notice of the weaknesses of those around us. It is not our goal to change others, but to understand them better as we are on our way to understanding ourselves better and living from a place of continuously and ever-evolving elevated consciousness. When we do this, we start to take accountability for where we are at in life and where we are headed. With this accountability, we realize it is our personal responsibility to create our own happiness and internal peace, and that it's never the job of someone else.

It is up to us to realize that the only person holding us back in life is our self. The victim mentality will begin to dissolve its supposed power over our lives. Obstacles, hurdles, and mountains will begin to appear less daunting—maybe even less frequent—and will be easier to navigate around.

Keep focused on where you're heading in life as this will help keep the road blocks transparent so they will not block the view of your path. When you are in a place of peace, you move beyond these with ease and grace.

When we connect to our faith, activate it, and feel the internal divine love, our surroundings will match. When we come from fear, we experience things that perpetuate the fear. When we live in joy, peace, and happiness, our worlds will mirror that back to us.

Zen Life Balance is about:

1. Recognizing where you are personally in this current moment (if you're satisfied or unsatisfied) and in which direction you *want* to head—that of satisfaction or dissatisfaction.
2. Quieting the mind and becoming aware of and accountable for how your thoughts, feelings, emotions, words, and actions bring about the balance and imbalance in your life. (Whether they bring you closer to or further away from what you want, which is ultimately to feel and experience a sense of peace and contentment)
3. Adjusting your thought focus according to the present awareness of the emotions you're experiencing.
4. Moving consistently forward in a way that will not only improve your life and bring forth a sense of peace and whatever else you desire, but will also be an inspiration to others.

Life is just a mirror reflecting our inner consciousness (awareness), emotions, and perceptions. Stand in front of the mirror of life and say, "I am worthy of peace, happiness, love, health, abundance, and everything my heart desires. And so it is!"

Let's begin this journey:

One day at a time.

One step at a time.

One thought at a time.

One emotion at a time.

One feeling at a time.

You get to choose how you want to feel every step of the way.

Give yourself permission to feel the way you mean
to feel regardless of the conditions,

or what anyone thinks, says or does.

CHAPTER 1

My Story

June 1999. I was in the doctor's office with my mom standing next to me, waiting for the results of the bloodwork. The doctor confirmed what the other doctor had said—leukemia. I was twenty-five at the time. My very first thought was, *Oh no, my poor mom. This is going to be so hard on her; she's going to worry and be sad.* My second thought was, *Wow, there must be some really good things that are going to happen in my life.* I didn't know that would've ever been something I would've thought about instantly upon getting a cancer diagnosis, yet the thought seemed to flow from me so naturally. My next thought, which I immediately vocalized, was to ask the doctor what we needed to do now. I had bills to pay, debt to continue working on, and a life to live.

I experienced doctor visits, bloodwork, pharmaceutical drugs, side effects that were so debilitating at times that I wasn't able to talk, severe and paralyzing anxieties and panic attacks, and amnesia. My skin literally peeled off if I brushed up against something gently. I was literally and figuratively falling apart as the years rolled on. I made a decision one day that I wasn't going to continue to live like this. I wondered what my body and quality of life would be like if I continued taking these drugs that were so toxic to my entire body. What did my future look like? It didn't seem good at all. How would my organs hold up? And the thought of what I'd have to go through with a bone marrow transplant was terrifying. Besides, they said that in my case it would be harder to find a donor to match close enough to have a successful outcome. Ha ha, go figure. I always did like to stand out in the crowd and didn't like conformity. So six years after my diagnosis, I decided one day that I was going to get off the drugs since I didn't like the side effects. I didn't know how this was going to happen or when, but I resolved to know that it would indeed happen. Of course, a few friends and family thought I was nuts and were worried that I would cause harm by stopping the drugs, but I knew that the answer to how this was going to happen would come in due time. I never wavered with the knowing, regardless of what anybody else thought or the current reality of my situation.

I began to create new daily habits and continued to cultivate my faith and belief of my body healing and not needing to be on the toxic drugs. I focused on what helped me to feel good even though I was still experiencing the side effects at the moment. I was already a personal trainer and knew many things about the health of the body, but it became apparent that being fit and being truly healthy were two different things altogether. In September 2005, I went to a routine visit with the doctor to go over my most recent bloodwork results, and he informed me that he was going to have me stop prescription drugs for a short period of time in order to bring my white blood cell count back up, as the numbers were low at the moment. He said it would be for a couple of weeks; he'd start me back up again when the cell counts were back up.

On our way out of town later that day, it suddenly dawned on me that my answer had come, and I knew that I would not go back to taking the drugs again. For the next two years, I went faithfully each month to have my bloodwork checked, and the numbers were staying stable. What I was doing (and not doing) in my daily life was actually working. Creating more balance and managing my stress was allowing my body to do what it was intended to do—heal under the right conditions. This is innate for all of us unless we block this from happening— mentally, emotionally, and physically.

In August 2007, my husband and I decided we were ready to plan to have a baby. I conceived the second month of trying. The first month of trying, I was a bit hesitant about the reality of having a baby, but the second month I was at ease about it. The birth was 100 percent natural and took about five hours. It's not to say that the stress of having a newborn didn't take its toll (which caused my white cell count to rise again), followed by the unexpected death of my mom a year later while on vacation out of the country, losing our house five months later due to foul play by the bank, and then the divorce two years after that. Whew! I did have to go back on the drugs again about two months after having my daughter, but I made the decision to get off them again after my divorce. I followed the same path that I had previously, with success.

Finding my balance in life and managing stress wasn't about having a stress-free life; it was about *choosing* to do that, creating a realistic plan of action, having consistent faith and belief in the process, never giving up, living mindfully, and personally growing every day.

This book came to be because of another very stressful time in my life. In July 2014, my boyfriend was hit head-on while riding a motorcycle because someone decided to pass other cars while on a two-lane road. He lost the use of his left arm and was in chronic, debilitating pain. After his third excruciating surgery, he was in recovery at home, lying in bed in the fetal position, not wanting to move, eat, or drink. I told him that if he felt like he'd gotten to a point where he wanted to end his life to please let me know so we could deal with that decision together. I had never seen someone in that immense amount of physical pain before, in which pain meds didn't help. At the same time, the person I worked for was quietly running the business into the ground, leaving me to explain to our fitness clients that I didn't know what was going on, but no matter what may or may not be happening, I would be there for them, and I wasn't going to leave.

Every day I drove to work for many miles on one of two two-lane roads. One had construction and delays; the other was the road that my boyfriend had been hit on. Neither was preferable. Diesel trucks traveled on these roads, and there were two days in a row that I remember clearly when I came to an understanding of how easy it would be to just veer in front of an oncoming truck in hopes of ending the heaviness of all I was experiencing. But I knew that would not be an acceptable or even an absolute solution, as death was not guaranteed. I could potentially create more problems, so I connected to my faith, listened to Wayne Dyer CDs, and knew that the feeling was only temporary and would lift soon. I had already started gathering the ideas for this book, so I picked up my notebook and put my focus back to adding more material to it. Within a day or two, I noticed how much better I was feeling. During the next six months or so, whenever I started feeling disconnected and overwhelmed, I would put my focus back on writing my book, and it seemed to help each time. My mood and overall outlook on life would become enjoyable again. I knew what I was putting together was working as long as I was being mindful and consistent with connecting to the material. I began to practice the tools every day because I wanted to feel as good as possible. I wanted the sense of peace to continue. I wanted to keep my mind from overthinking. I wanted to focus more on the things in life that were bringing happiness to me instead of the things that created chaos and stress. I wanted to keep my mind focused on the thoughts that caused me to feel good. As I did this more consistently, I noticed more things happening in my life that were a match to how good I was feeling. And with consistent practice, I am able to keep myself in a good-feeling place and connect with good-feeling circumstances more of the time. I'm also able to catch myself quickly when my mind begins to veer off track, run amuck, and focus on thoughts that don't serve my well-being.

I feel very blessed and appreciative to have found this insight. And I'm very happy to pass this along so that you can empower yourself and live a truly enjoyable and amazing life.

***

Zen Life Balance is a journey, not a destination. We must never stop. Life becomes easier to navigate, more fulfilling, more enjoyable, and more peaceful. You'll wonder why you didn't do this sooner, but you'll be even more appreciative that you are doing it now.

***

- What do you desire in your life at the moment?

- How do you want to feel on a regular basis (e.g., satisfied, optimistic, peaceful, passionate, happy, empowered, loved)?

CHAPTER 2

I Am / I See Myself Being ...

The "I am" statement is about the thoughts, words, actions, feelings, and habits that build the beliefs you have come to live with about yourself and your life that you would like to affirm or change. These are two of the most powerful words because what you put after them shapes your reality. For each tool in the book, you'll be completing an "I am" sentence. Start here with whatever comes to mind. Write the goal in the present tense and in a positive way. If it is something that may be a stretch for you to believe at the moment, you can use the phrase "I see myself being able to ..."

I am: I see myself being able to forgive easily and effortlessly.

I am healthy, whole and complete.

I am: I am happy in all my relationships.

I am successful and always heading in the right direction.

I am: I see myself being financially abundant. Money comes to me from all directions.

I am: My soul is filled with the blessing of abundant love. I am loved. I am love.

I am: _____

I am: _____

I am: _____

I am: _____

I am: _____

I am: _____

I am: _____

I am: _____

I am: _____

I am: _____

I am: _____

I am: _____

I am: _____

CHAPTER 3

Meditate

- To relax and disconnect (quiet your mind) from thoughts and emotions that aren't serving your highest good so that you can reconnect to a state of being that allows you to regain your alignment to thoughts and emotions that benefit you, as well as those around you.
- Get comfortable (sit or lay down). It's recommended you close your eyes, but you could also focus on an object like a candle or salt lamp. If you can, have a fan on that makes a constant noise or find a sound app. The goal is to do this daily for about fifteen minutes or more in the morning to set the stage for the unfolding day. When we are relaxed and connected to our divine self, we have the ability to connect with what is a match to that. The other people and things that would normally throw us off our course will either not bother us or not be present in our experience.
- Breathing with intention and on purpose is a way to meditate in the midst of any condition that might be distracting you away from your true nature of being satisfied and happy. Close your mouth and focus on the breath going deep into your body via your nose. When you're lungs are full, slowly exhale through your nose or mouth until you feel like you can't stand it any longer and are naturally guided to breathe deeply again. You can do this anywhere at any time—even while driving your car.

I Am: _____

- Another way to reconnect to your divine self through meditation is to turn your thoughts to things around you that stimulate good feelings and by appreciating what's going on around you. Notice trees and flowers, chirping birds, dogs being walked, beautiful colors, the clouds, or whatever is near that helps you feel uplifted.

- Drive to the ocean or somewhere where there is water like a waterfall or fountain, or even a pond. There was a time when I needed to calm my mind by driving to the ocean to sit and stare at the water and listen to the crashing of the waves. I did this two days in a row, and it helped tremendously. Water is very calming for me. In fact, I sleep with an app running so I can listen to a soothing forest creek all night.

- There are many ways to meditate throughout the day: doing dishes, vacuuming, yoga, stretching, taking a nap, going for a walk, listening to music, or just sit and be satisfied for fifteen to twenty minutes.

- Don't look for answers during meditation; look for detachment. The answers you seek will come to you in moments when you're not focused on the problem(s), when you otherwise happily occupy your time and attention.

➔ In addition to a morning meditation, find other ways through the day that help to keep your mind at ease:

_____

_____

_____

_____

CHAPTER 4

Love

- unconditionally
- without barriers and expectations
- love yourself first!

    Love comes from within before it can be returned.

- The love you'll allow into your life is equivalent to the love you have for yourself (the amount, the genuineness).
- Love everything as it is, not as it could be (that's conditional).
- Love yourself and someone else as they are, not who you think they could be, should be, or have the potential to be. If you place conditions on love, you will always find more conditions to place ahead of love. Let go of unnecessary expectations when it comes to love. Allow love to be; it cannot be forced or directed.
- Putting conditions on love may be a way to protect your vulnerability, even protecting you against yourself.
- Love from your inner spirit, soul, and heart.
- Relationships:

    Love me without fear

    Trust me without questioning

    Need me without restrictions

    Accept me without change

    Desire me without inhibitions

    For a love so free

    Will never fly away …

I am: _____

➔ What things do you notice in your day that inspire love in you? What acts of love do you notice around you? Take notice, and feel the love. Write down what you observe then come back to it later and connect how you feel about what you observed. Love is all around us in people holding doors open for others, kind words, letting someone in during traffic, smiling at someone, and so forth.

_____

_____

_____

_____

_____

_____

_____

_____

_____

_____

_____

_____

- You are a creature of Divine Love connected at all times to Source. Divine Love is when you see God in everyone and everything you encounter."

—Wayne Dyer

- When you see someone (including yourself) through the eyes of love, you'll be less likely to judge, criticize, and find fault.
- Love is passionate, not indifferent.
  Love is selfless, not self-serving (self-centered).
  Love is freedom, not possession.
  Love empowers all.
  Love has no time limits.
- "Love in its purest form is a sharing of joy. It asks nothing in return, it expects nothing; hence, how could you feel hurt? When you don't expect, there is no possibility of being hurt. Then whatsoever comes is good, and if nothing comes, then that is good. Your joy was to give, not to get." —Osho
- Love by definition:
  —A profoundly tender, passionate affection (for the self and others)
  —affectionate concern for the well-being of others
  —the benevolent affection for people, animals, things, places
- ➔ Practice daily, random acts of love and kindness toward others (uplifting notes, letting someone in during traffic, holding the door open for someone, saying hi to a stranger, or even just a smile).
- ➔ Aim to do at least one act of kindness each day without anyone knowing and without any expectation of acknowledgment. And take time daily to show love for yourself (take a bath, a workout, massage, cup of tea, nap, whatever works for you).

➜ If there is anything you would like to shift in regard to yourself, seek that strength out in others. Make note of what you are seeking in others and wanting to transform in yourself. Know that you are now causing a shift internally as you love and appreciate these qualities in others.

_____

_____

_____

_____

_____

_____

_____

_____

_____

_____

_____

_____

_____

_____

_____

_____

_____

"Love as though you have never been hurt before."

—Souza

- There are many different levels of love when it comes to love for self, love for others, and accepting love. We are always in a state of being able to bring about an increase of love to our consciousness. In our relationships, it can come from taking time to understand the other person and what it means for them to feel loved. Love is something we show and demonstrate, not just something we say out of habit. Are you showing love in a way that truly conveys how you feel? This includes the love that you show yourself.

- To accept the love we desire, we must be willing to love ourselves first as this creates a ground floor from which the love will build, grow, and multiply. If we deny our own love by constantly giving it away to others, we are leaving our own self with a void. And when love is shown to us, it won't fill us up if we haven't built a stable foundation of self-love, so the love seems temporary and maybe even unfulfilling. We cannot adequately give away what we do not have ourselves. And we cannot truly accept it from others when we deny our own self-love first.

- We experience love because we make the choice to feel it.

- No matter how we feel about ourselves at the moment or how we perceive others feel about us, our divine self loves us more! Feel the comfort in this.

- "Love is the ability and willingness to allow those you care for to be what they choose for themselves without any insistence that they satisfy you."
  —Wayne Dyer

➔ In your close personal relationships, slow down to observe the things you love. With the ones we see all the time it can be easier to block out what we love and get caught up focusing on the frustrations. See your world through the eyes of love; see past the surface. When you swim in the pool of anything but love, you will see, feel, and experience anything but love. What pool are you swimming in?

➔ If today was the last day ever for you to see someone you love, would you perhaps take the time to see all that you love in them? Do that now.

_____

_____

_____

_____

_____

_____

_____

_____

_____

_____

_____

_____

_____

_____

"We accept the love we think we deserve."

—Stephen Chbosky

CHAPTER 5

Appreciation

- Do you appreciate yourself, others, things, circumstances, life?
- Bring the best of you to every experience in life. Put appreciation ahead of you wherever you go, and you will experience things, situations, people, and a life that will confirm your appreciation. Bring doubt with you, and that's what you'll experience. Bring anger or sorrow with you, and you will experience more of that as well.
- → Be appreciative of the little things first—the things that tend to get overlooked every day.
- Start your day with appreciation, and end it with appreciation.
- Find ways to be grateful for experiences in your life that have brought about change and allowed you to get to a better place.
- Are you grateful to be alive each day, or do you take your life for granted?
- Are you appreciative of your relationship, family, children, career? What about money, health, happiness, love, and so forth?
- → Give thanks out loud. Say thank you every day for every little thing you are appreciative of in the moment; don't wait. Do not be afraid or hesitate to say thank you.
- Appreciation changes everything! Accept each moment, and be appreciative of wherever you are at in life and what you are learning. After all, that's exactly what happiness is: accepting, learning, growing, allowing.

I am: _____

➜ What/who are you appreciative of in your life (things, people, experiences)? Take notice of everything from the seemingly small to the obvious things. When you see or even think about the people and things you are appreciative of, how does that feel? Speak your appreciation out loud every day to the people you come across, and even say thank you out loud when you are alone.

_____

_____

_____

_____

_____

_____

_____

_____

_____

_____

_____

_____

_____

"We tend to see what we expect to see. How can we feel good
when we expect to see/experience things that don't feel good?
Instead, expect to see/experience things that feel good."
—Darlene Alisa

CHAPTER 6

Believe (Belief System)

- Whatever you believe will be true for you.
- Beliefs start when we're very young and can be passed down through generations. Think about what you believe in all areas of your life as you go through your day. Get curious about everything you believe.
- The key is to become the observer of your thoughts and actions, and then challenge your beliefs behind them.
- Believe that anything is possible. Anything is possible if you believe.
- Instead of saying, "I'll believe it when I see it," say, "I'll see it when I believe it."
- Believe that poor health isn't inevitable or incurable.
- "Natural forces within us are the true healers of disease." —Hippocrates
- Beliefs are simply repeated thoughts with strong feelings attached to them (e.g. I find it hard to lose weight or my family suffers from poor health, so I will too).
- Beliefs are stronger than just speaking the words. Those are two separate things that must be in alignment in order to create change (e.g. simply stating that you'd like to be in a relationship but actually believing relationships create stress or that you'll lose your independence will interfere with attracting a partner. You may even attract a partner that leads to a stressful relationship or someone who doesn't value individual freedom).

I am: _____

➜ Know what you know (in all areas of life) and then question why you believe that. What are your beliefs about love, happiness, finances, health, spirituality, religion, family, career, success, and so forth? Where did that belief come from? Who did it come from? Does it still serve a purpose? If not, develop a new belief that supports your desires in life.

My Current Belief   **My Updated Belief**

_____

_____

_____

_____

_____

_____

_____

_____

_____

_____

_____

_____

"If you believe it will work out, you'll see opportunities.
If you believe it won't, you will see obstacles."

—Wayne Dyer

"As you believe, and so it is."

—Darlene Alisa

CHAPTER 7

Stress Management
(Let Go, Surrender, Release Control)

- Stress (physical, mental, emotional) is part of life. How we perceive it and either *react* based on past experiences or *respond* based on the current moment will determine our joy in life, as well as our health.
- Disease is a result of a lack of ease in the body for a long period of time—stress, worry, fear.
- *Your emotions affect every cell in the body.* Mental, emotional, and physical are all intertwined.
- The more we try to actively control situations, people, and outcomes, the more frustration, tension, and chaos we tend to create and experience.
- By letting go and surrendering and responding rather than reacting, we can discover a whole new side to ourselves.
- *The only thing we have control of in life is how we respond to what happens (attitude), the thoughts we focus on, and our perceptions.* Life is how we think it is.
- If you begin to stress about something or someone, recognize it and realize that your job isn't to make things happen. *Your job is to quiet your mind, keep yourself centered, remember what the end goal is, and to allow things to come together;* it seems that whenever we reflect back on stressful times, we see a pattern that things have a tendency of working out for the greater good of everyone.

I am: _____

➜ Recognize and make note of when you are trying to control a situation, person, or outcome and if there is tension or ease surrounding this. Become the observer of yourself in your life.

_____

_____

_____

_____

_____

_____

_____

_____

_____

_____

_____

_____

_____

_____

_____

"To be calm is the highest achievement of the self."

—Zen proverb

"Sometimes letting things go is an act of far greater power than defending or hanging on."

—Eckhart Tolle

- Our strength will always be equivalent to what we need in any given situation.

- *Surrender what you have no control over.* Put your hands up and ask for help. Hand it over to Spirit, who always knows the answer. Ask the question you would like the answer to. Ask to be given a sign or direction when things get stressful and you don't have a solution. *Overthinking, complaining, worrying, lying awake at night, and becoming bitter or depressed will not solve anything.* Releasing control and surrendering is not about giving up; it's about recognizing that you don't have a solution and that you're willing to open yourself up so that one can be presented to you.

- *If you're controlled by your circumstances—up when things are up, down when things don't go your way—life is going to be a roller coaster and very chaotic.*

- We must not let our circumstances determine whether or not we're going to be happy. "I'm not going to allow what's happening on the outside to get on the inside."

➔ "Dedicate a week to charting incidents of things working out without you having to control or make them happen. This will mean consciously choosing situations where you curb your automatic impulses to control the outcome. Relax when you want to tense up, and trust in as many situations as you can. At the end of the week, notice how changing the way you think has changed your life."

—Wayne Dyer

➜ Practice surrendering your desire to control the when, how, and who to allow the mind, body, and spirit to align with your desires. Recognize when you are about to activate the control part of you and pull it back. This takes practice. Write down when you got frustrated in a situation but were able to pull back the control factor and allow things to fall into place.

_____

_____

_____

_____

_____

_____

_____

_____

_____

_____

_____

_____

_____

_____

_____

"A wise man, recognizing that the world is but an illusion,
does not act as if it is real, so he escapes the suffering."

—Buddha

- There's nothing the world can throw at you that can hold you down without your consent—nothing.
- Decide to have a good day, and so it shall be.
- If you found out you only had three months to live, would you let the same things that stressed you out last week stress you out this week?
- Develop a no-worries attitude. Worry less; trust more.
- *Focus on what you can control, not what you can't.* Learn to recognize the difference. Release control and surrender in the moment you realize you have little to no control over the situation.
- We do have control over our thoughts, perceptions, emotions, our feelings, our responses, our attitude, and our actions. *We do not have control over others, what they say, what they choose to do, what they choose to believe.*
- Do not waste time and energy trying to change things we cannot change, as this only adds to the chaos that may be going on.
- Move in a different direction; change the focus.
- When you recognize that you need to let go and surrender, realize that the right people and circumstances already exist and will show up on time.
- We are blind to the solution when we are engulfed in, committed to talking about, and frustrated with the problem.
- When you try to control everything, you enjoy nothing. Relax, breathe, let go, and allow! Then the solution will present itself.

→ When a stressful thought or situation arises (kids, job, significant other, and so forth), recognize your initial unconscious reaction. Did you take it personally? Were you trying to control an outcome or another person? Did you have an expectation that wasn't met and feel let down or angry? Learn to release expectations of *how* something should occur and focus on what you actually want to have happen in the end. Take a moment to think about if what you're going to say or do will bring about a positive outcome or create more stress, tension, and drama. *Reacting* is far too automated and leads to tension instead of a solution. *Responding* takes into consideration all the components of a situation, leaves the emotion behind, and allows for a more positive outcome.

→ For everything that weighs on you and stresses you out, complete the next two pages. This will help you recognize if you have direct control over your stress or if you need to practice releasing control and surrendering. Fill these pages out for each individual stressful situation.

"By releasing control over circumstances, you
gain more control over your life."

—Kyle Maynard

- There is nothing to worry about—ever! Either you have control or you don't. If you do, then take control. If you don't, then dismiss it for the moment. Don't waste your energy on worry. What is your stress? ➔Go to the next page. If you don't have control, then surrender and practice what is listed below ⬇. If you do have control, then list the steps necessary to alleviate the stress ➔

Either way, we ultimately learn that we are always in control of our thoughts, emotions, words, and actions, regardless of the situation.

➔ Breathe
➔ Relax
➔ Connect with your faith
➔ Pray
➔ Meditate (quiet your mind)
➔ Believe that it is already resolved
➔ Know the solution is being delivered (even though you haven't seen it yet)
➔ Trust and let go
➔ Come from a place of love within
➔ Ask for the answer or direction to be shown
➔ Play! Laugh! Have Fun!
➔ Whatever feels good: _____
➔ _____
➔ _____
➔ _____

→ What is my stress? What outcome would I like, or how would I prefer to feel instead, regardless of the situation?

_____

_____

_____

_____

_____

_____

→ List the logical steps that are *within your control* to alleviate the stress or steps to change your perception of the stress.

☐ _____

☐ _____

☐ _____

☐ _____

☐ _____

☐ _____

☐ _____

☐ _____

☐ _____

☐ _____

- Let go of comparing.
- Let go of justifying.
- Let go of judgments.
- Let go of complaining.
- Let go of regrets.
- Let go of blame.
- Let go of fear.
- Let go of guilt.
- Let go of worrying.
- Let go of anger.
- Laugh!

➔ What would I like to let go of that isn't serving me? What would I like to practice instead?

_____

_____

_____

_____

_____

_____

_____

_____

_____

_____

_____

_____

_____

_____

_____

_____

"Let go of your ego's need to be right."

—Wayne Dyer

"Only by letting go and not caring what others think, will you
find the freedom to embrace and be your own unique self."

—Darlene Alisa

CHAPTER 8

Forgiveness

- Allows internal freedom and peace and lightens your spirit.
- When we forgive, we do not erase the memory, we simply choose to free ourselves from the feelings of bitterness, hurt, anger, resentment, disappointment, and emotional or physical distress.
- Every situation that calls for forgiveness allows us to learn more about ourselves and others and to personally grow, which leads to healing mentally, emotionally and physically.
- Forgiveness allows us to move forward in life and love instead of being stuck replaying the old scenario over and over and reliving the feelings, in turn creating mental and emotional frustration and illness.
- Focus on the clarity you gained, your strength, and your tenacity.
- To hold resentment creates inflammation in the body that can manifest as disease.
- How do you forgive, let it go, or move on? You stop reviving it and giving it energy. The emotional attachment to the person or event will fade out over time and no longer affect you.
- Stop replaying the old scenario over and over in your head.
- There is personal power and freedom in forgiving and allowing yourself to move forward.
- It's not up to us to handle past grievances, errors, and conflicts or to hold a grudge by claiming resentment, anger, and misery toward our self or others. All that we go through is to help us get where we want to go, but not letting go holds us back.
- Set your pride aside and see the value instead of the hurt.

I am: _____

→ Forgiveness starts with the self first, as this process begins within and isn't necessarily about verbally involving the other person, as they have most likely moved on long ago. Forgiveness is about moving forward and letting go of the emotional heaviness (baggage) that is weighing you down. Look for examples of forgiveness in others in your day as a way to begin. Recognizing that you're holding on to something that is affecting you emotionally and physically is the first part of forgiveness. The second part is the action of letting go and choosing to focus on something more satisfying. It becomes easier with practice.

_____

_____

_____

_____

_____

_____

_____

_____

_____

_____

"Forgiveness is the final form of love."
—Reinhold Niebuhr

➜ Recognition is about making a conscious connection to how you feel emotionally and physically when you hold resentment and continue to own it, whether it's from the current moment or from the past. The action part is about not waiting for the other person to change but about changing the way you see things in the current moment and changing your perceptions and responses to what appears to be weighing on you from the past (even five minutes ago).

What am I releasing?   **What is even the slightest more satisfying thing to focus on?**

_____

_____

_____

_____

_____

_____

_____

_____

_____

_____

_____

_____

_____

_____

_____

When I release the hurt and pain, how does it feel?

(lighter, a sense of peace, freedom, less tension and heaviness)

_____

_____

_____

_____

_____

_____

_____

What am I observing in my interactions with others, my own emotions, and how am I looking at life now that I have started to forgive and move forward? (ease and flow, more enjoyment, and so forth)

_____

_____

_____

_____

_____

_____

_____

CHAPTER 9

Enjoyable Exercise

- The best exercise program ever designed is the one you'll actually do, the one you enjoy doing, the one that causes you to feel better mentally and physically, the one that resonates with the lifestyle that you either have or would like to have, the one that continues to progress your fitness levels on a realistic level.
- Your body is like a three-year-old child. If at any point you make them do something they don't want to do or don't enjoy doing over and over, you will most certainly get resistance and/or non-compliance. If you force yourself to run when you know you don't like running or go to a gym that you don't enjoy, you will most likely not get the results you want. But if you have the *desire* to run, then it is important to keep practicing so as to get better at it as it may take some time to become second nature.
- Commit to extra physical activity more days than not (four to six days a week).
- Concentrate on consistency over intensity and length of time to begin. Once you establish a habit most days of the week, then increase the time.
- Work up to thirty to sixty minutes a day.
- Walk your dog or ask a neighbor if you can walk theirs.
- The goal of adequate exercise is to get yourself out of your current fitness level and challenge yourself.
→ Challenge and stretch your muscles every day!
- Working on flexibility and range of motion has the power to keep the joints free from unnecessary stress and tension. What appears to be a knee problem may be nothing more than a shortened, tight tendon or ligament that could become a problem if not addressed.

I am: _____

➔ Start today. Go for a fifteen minute walk. Stretch daily. Experience how something so simple changes the way you feel mentally, physically, and emotionally. Add ten to twenty pushups daily. Do these against the kitchen or bathroom counter, if needed.

➔ Jot down how you feel today: your mood, energy level, sleep patterns, how you feel in the morning, midday, and evening. Record how you feel after taking a walk, stretching, or simply doing a few pushups.

_____

_____

_____

_____

_____

_____

_____

_____

_____

_____

_____

_____

_____

"Be grateful for the body you have as it has gotten you this far and is taking you to achieve your goals. Enjoy the journey. Be excited for all the things you are learning about yourself."

—Darlene Alisa

CHAPTER 10

Balanced Nutrition / Intuitive Eating

- Drink eight to sixteen ounces of water upon waking and half your body weight in ounces every day, with the goal of increasing this amount to adequately hydrate, cleanse the body, and prevent a disruption in metabolic processes and brain function.
- Lack of water and sleep can drive unnecessary hunger.
- Every cell in our body requires water to function, and without the proper amount, our bodies simply cannot function properly. Our bodies ache, heads hurt, we forget things, and we get tired and irritable. We think we're hungry, but really our cells are thirsty.
- Have a plan for your day that includes time to eat. Winging it and not prioritizing giving nourishment to your body will most likely cause you to overeat or choose unbeneficial foods.
- Eat food that comes in its natural form rather than processed food whenever possible. Our bodies digest food from nature more efficiently, helping us to feel more satisfied. Be mindful when eating.
- → Pay attention to your emotions and mood before and about thirty to sixty minutes after you eat. How does the food or drink make your body feel? Are you energized or sluggish, happy or depressed, satisfied or still hungry?
- → Pay attention to the circumstances that drive you to eat or drink. Is food or drink your reward? Does it calm you when you're stressed? Would there be another way to deal with stress? When you're hungry, is it your brain or your stomach that drives your hunger? If you feel stress may be the driving force in your eating, then refer to the stress management (release control, surrender) tool.

I am: _____

→ Do I carry any guilt with me regarding food?

→ Ask yourself, "Am I eating to nourish my body and brain or to fill a void, to make me feel better because I'm stressed out (a temporary fix)?"

→ When the body needs water it will signal hunger. Start by drinking water first, then give it about twenty minutes.

_____

_____

_____

_____

_____

_____

_____

_____

_____

_____

_____

_____

_____

_____

_____

"Let food be thy medicine and medicine be thy food."

—Hippocrates

CHAPTER 11

Restorative Sleep

- This is your daily emotional reset button.
- ↓cortisol & adrenaline, ↑HGH (growth hormone) that repairs and grows new tissue.
- This is when the body repairs and rebuilds from all the daily damage that occurs from wear and tear, exercise, environmental, mental, emotional, and physical stress.
- Revs up your metabolism and regulates your hunger hormones. Keeps your waistline down and your appetite in check.
- It's not about how little you think you can *survive* on; it's about getting the amount and quality that allows you to *thrive*.
- Your immune system will work better.
- Your brain will be cleaner, as neurotoxins will be cleared out. Memory will improve.
- Feel better emotionally, mentally, and physically.
- Better control with eating.
- Better overall health: less chance for high blood pressure, strokes and heart attacks, diabetes and any other inflammatory diseases.
- → Limit bright lights—including computers and phones—and activity near bedtime as these are stimulating to the brain and body and can disrupt the deep sleep patterns.
- → Limit or do away with caffeine after lunch.

I am: _____

➜ How many hours of sleep are you currently getting? Do you feel refreshed when you wake up or tired and irritated?

➜ Create a calming routine in the evening close to bedtime. For example, you can make a cup of herbal tea, read, take a bath, stretch, meditate, and breathe.

➜ Talking about the news or the worries of the world will create tension in the body and weigh heavily on the mind. Instead, turn your focus to things that allow you to feel good and instill a sense of peace all day and near bedtime.

_____

_____

_____

_____

_____

_____

_____

_____

_____

_____

_____

"I put my head on the pillow & let the stillness put
things where they are supposed to be."

—Darlene Alisa

CHAPTER 12

Identify Your Happy

- *You* are responsible for your own happiness. It is never anybody's job to make you happy, nor can anyone keep you from being happy. This is an inside job.
- ➜ Decide to be happy, and so it is!
- ➜ Pay attention to your current focus of thoughts and perceptions of recent or past interactions or experiences. Shift your focus away from the thoughts that tend to keep you in a negative space. Spend more time with the positive thoughts, and positive things will become more apparent to you.
- ➜ Be observant of the situations, ways of thinking, habits and rituals that help harbor internal or external chaos and tension. Recognize your current emotional state and shift your focus to more enjoyable thoughts, or take a moment to do something positive that helps disrupt the pattern of thought.
- ➜ Give more energy and attention to the thoughts, things, people, and circumstances that inspire you, uplift you, and allow your heart and soul to smile.
- "The greater part of our happiness or misery depends upon our dispositions and not our circumstances." —Martha Washington
- "We tend to forget that happiness doesn't come as a result of getting something we don't have, but rather of recognizing and appreciating what we do have." —Frederick Keonig
- Again, make a decision to be happy, and so it is!

I am: _____

→ Start noticing during the day if or when there are shifts in your energy from feeling positive, energized, and upbeat to feeling negative and drained.

→ Can you change the circumstances (probably not), or do you need to change your attitude and perception of the moment? Pretending to be happy will not suffice here.

→ Even if your life isn't where you'd like it to be, create pockets of happy moments throughout the day as frequently as possible.

→ "Happiness will never come to those who fail to appreciate what they already have. Happiness does not depend on what you have or who you are; it solely relies on what you think." —Buddha

_____

_____

_____

_____

_____

_____

_____

_____

"Success is not the key to happiness.
Happiness is the key to success."

—Albert Schweitzer

"There is no path to Happiness. Happiness is the path."

—Buddha

CHAPTER 13

Quiet Your Mind

- Our perception of situations, circumstances, or people will either create internal and external peace or chaos. This one goes with stress management.
- → *Pay attention to what you're paying attention to.* When we take notice of what we're focusing our attention on, we can decide if it's actually productive or if we need to redirect our thoughts.
- → Notice when your mind starts running amuck. Are you jumping to conclusions without all the facts? Are you creating a conversation in your mind as if you're certain about future events, interactions, conversations, or outcomes that have not happened? If you don't have all the information, you may be impatient and try to fill in the blanks with improper facts instead of the truth.
- → Is the internal conversation based on the current truth, or is it from past experiences? Be present in the current moment.
- → Ask yourself, *Why am I quick to think this way in this situation? What benefit would there be in thinking this way?*
- Whatever is going on around you is just a projection of your own mind, feelings, inner emotions, and beliefs. Step back, breathe.
- Your mind will tell you all the reasons something good is not going to happen based on fear, not on the truth.
- → When your mind is racing, take a moment to breathe slowly, either while closing your eyes or focusing on something pleasing, until you feel some relief.
- → Repeat: "Things are always working out for me."

I am: _____

_____

_____

_____

_____

_____

_____

_____

_____

_____

_____

_____

_____

_____

_____

_____

_____

_____

"Quiet the mind and allow the whispers
of the Universe to be heard."

—Darlene Alisa

- Our minds want to make logical sense of things, such as figuring out the details of how something is going to happen. This is when we must quiet our minds and tap into our faith (whatever that may be for each of us).
- The things we see and experience are temporary. They will change when we quiet our minds and change our thoughts to the things we want to see and experience—things that feel good.
- You can give a negative thought significance in your mind and convince yourself that you should indeed be unhappy, irritated, angry, disappointed, discouraged, resentful, guilty, fearful, or sad. Or you can recognize that your mind is about to create a mental landslide, and you can choose to dismiss the thought altogether and focus on a better-feeling one.
- Sometimes you have to quit thinking so much. If it feels right, it probably is. So just go with it. This is using your intuition, your gut feeling.
- "A bird sitting on a tree is never afraid of the branch breaking because her trust is not on the branch but on her own wings, her ability to fly." —Wayne Dyer
- *Believe in yourself.* Quiet your mind and have faith and a knowing that it is all working as it should. Take it one step at a time.
- Silence your ego and need for control, and your power will arise. Be mindful that your daily conversations aren't continuing to add fuel to your busy mind chatter, anxiety, and negativity.

_____

_____

_____

_____

_____

_____

_____

_____

_____

_____

_____

_____

_____

_____

_____

_____

_____

_____

_____

_____

_____

"Quiet your mind and your soul will speak."

– Ma Jaya Sati

CHAPTER 14

Self Introspection

- When we reflect on how we think, feel, and act, we bring about the opportunity for personal growth. As such, we also bring about experiences with ourselves and others that are more positive and more favorable, rather than continuing to experience unwanted situations.
- → Reflect upon interactions with others, your day, how you handled a situation, your behavior, and your automated habits.
- → Pay attention to how your thoughts, actions, words, behaviors, and habits affect others around you, as well as yourself. We can't change the past, but we can use every situation as a tool for personal growth.
- We cannot change others directly, but when we make even a slight alteration to our thoughts, actions, words, behaviors, and habits, it changes how others respond to us.
- → Reflect upon and decide what you will let go of in your day-to-day life in areas where you desire a change (i.e., frustrating morning or evening rituals with the kids, arguments that you keep having with your significant other, or leaving late and getting mad at being late due to traffic). This is taking personal responsibility for the physical and emotional energy that is being put forth instead of blaming others.
- It is important to reflect when you are in a positive or neutral state of mind to avoid blaming others or feeling guilty for how you handled a situation.

"Life can only be understood backwards,
but it must be lived forwards."

—Soren Kierkegaard

I am: _____

_____

_____

_____

_____

_____

_____

_____

_____

_____

_____

_____

_____

_____

_____

_____

"With everything that has happened to you, you can either
feel sorry for yourself or treat what has happened as a gift.
Everything is either an opportunity to grow or an obstacle
to keep you from growing. You get to choose."

—Wayne Dyer

CHAPTER 15

Be Present

- *Be observant.* Be present in the current moment.
- Observe the actions of others, not just their words.
- People won't tell you who they are. They'll show you—again and again.
- → *When you are in a conversation with someone, be present.* When you are too busy in your head, rushing, multi-tasking while trying to listen, anticipating what you'll say next instead of intently listening to what the other person is actually saying, you miss the topic or the point they are trying to get across.
- → Quiet your mind and practice just being present, with no expectations or agenda. Practice being flexible in the moment and going with the flow of things.
- → Observe the words of the songs you like and are drawn to. Are they positive or negative? Do they inspire you?
- → Observe the conversations you regularly engage in. Are they positive or negative? Are they productive or are they focused on what's going wrong?
- Look past what seems obvious. Don't be oblivious to what's going on around you.
- → Notice how your actions, behaviors, and words affect others.
- → Practice being present with your children and others close to you. Decide ahead of time to allow yourself to be in the moment with the most important people in your life instead of being sidetracked or distracted. Put the phone down and turn the TV off if necessary. Make eye contact with the other person.

I am: _____

_____

_____

_____

_____

_____

_____

_____

_____

_____

_____

_____

_____

_____

_____

_____

_____

_____

_____

_____

Everything we need to know is going on right in front of our eyes.

CHAPTER 16

Communicate with Intention

- Speak honestly but with kindness.
- Have integrity. Say what you mean, and mean what you say.
➜ Before you speak, THINK:
  T—is it True?
  H—is it Helpful?
  I—is it Inspiring?
  N—is it Necessary?
  K—is it Kind?
- Speak with intent to create a positive outcome through your words.
➜ Really figure out what your point is when you communicate with someone. What is the ultimate goal of the conversation, and what you would like to say? Be cautious not to get distracted with unnecessary details or emotions that may arise. Always return to thinking about the ultimate goal. Choosing your words wisely and being as clear as possible will help. Telling someone that you miss them and would love to spend more time with them comes across in a positive way versus telling that same person that you never see them anymore or insisting that they are avoiding you or that you're irritated that they're busy all the time.
- Communicating with someone is very different than talking to (or at) someone. Have you listened to what they have said and then responded to what they said, or did you instantly hijack the conversation with your story, experience, or agenda, only to put the focus on you? Take time and ask them questions about what they just said.

I am: _____

_____

_____

_____

_____

_____

_____

_____

_____

_____

_____

_____

_____

_____

_____

_____

_____

"When you're in the middle of an argument, ask yourself: Do I
want to be right or be happy? When you choose the joyous, loving,
spiritual mode, your connection to intention is strengthened."

—Wayne Dyer

- Whatever you keep repeating and saying over and over, you'll keep reinforcing within your mind (e.g., I am having a bad day. I am not good enough. This is just my lot in life.).

➔ Don't use your words to describe the situation, use your words to change the situation. Use your words to describe things as you would like the outcome to be. It is OK to say that you are having a challenging day, but if you follow that with saying you are still blessed and of the knowing that things are already turning positive. Refer back to your positive "I am" affirmations and declarations.

➔ Instead of talking or complaining about the way it is, talk about the way you want it to be. Talk about it in the present tense or that you know it is in the process of happening, and you're just not caught up in the details as they have already been worked out.

➔ Before offering advice to someone you are listening to, ask yourself whether they are actually asking for your opinion, or are you assuming they need you to tell them what to do just because they shared something with you?

➔ Pause before you initiate a conversation or respond to someone in order to take account of your current mood. Could what you're about to say create a positive or negative situation (for yourself or others)?

➔ Choose the path of least resistance (the one that feels better).

_____

_____

_____

_____

_____

_____

_____

_____

_____

_____

_____

_____

_____

_____

_____

_____

_____

_____

_____

"The single biggest problem in communication
is the illusion that it has taken place."

—George Bernard Shaw

➜ Be cautious. Your words may say one thing, but your actions and behaviors may be saying something completely different. We communicate in all sorts of ways, not just verbally. Actions and behaviors speak volumes. Make sure yours match your words. If you feel the need to explain yourself to others frequently, it is most likely because your words, actions, and habits are not in alignment or you may not be in acceptance of yourself and are trying to get approval or prove yourself through words instead of through your character. (See the **acceptance** tool.)

➜ Each day, make note of when you become aware of your mood and words, how you adjust yourself, and how that changes the usual outcome of a situation. This works great with children and family in the rush of the morning and the end of the evening.

_____

_____

_____

_____

_____

_____

_____

_____

_____

_____

_____

_____

_____

_____

_____

_____

_____

_____

_____

_____

_____

_____

_____

_____

_____

_____

_____

_____

"Let children read whatever they want and then talk about it
with them. If parents and kids can talk together, we won't have
as much censorship because we won't have as much fear."

—Judy Blume

CHAPTER 17

Connect with Your Spiritual Nature (Faith)

- Connect with your spiritual beliefs (i.e., your faith) every day.
- Whatever you believe in spiritually should bring about a sense of peace when you connect with that energy.
- → Reaffirm this connection daily through prayer, meditation, music, reading, affirmations, or seeing the beauty of nature.
- Your spiritual nature comes from within. It's not something you can see, but when you connect with it, you resonate with and are drawn to things outside of yourself that bring a sense of peace. For some it might look like going to church, jogging in the park, walking the dog, meditating, being at the ocean (or any sort of flowing water), and so many more things.
- When you are disconnected from your inner spirit, you may notice more chaos being drawn to you or you to it.
- If you're not sure where your beliefs are, then simply connecting to nature will help your spiritual connection and is a great way to start. Go for a walk, listen to the birds, look at the clouds. What color is the sky? Check out all that is going on around you.
- Your spiritual nature, faith, and beliefs are personal to you, and it is OK if they are different from someone else. The important thing is that you stay connected to the things that bring peace and contentment to your inner spirit and that allow you to be aligned with your highest self.
- Even when you think you can't, turn up your inner faith. This will remind you that you still can and always could when you needed to.

I am: _____

→ Each day, look to see the sunrise or the sunset.

→ What or who are you spiritually connected to? What feeds your soul? Your spiritual connection helps to quiet your mind and brings about a sense of ease and calm. Source Energy, the universe, nature, the ocean, mountains, spiritual centers or churches, meditation, support groups, and so forth can help you feel a sense of inner peace, joy, and contentment—a feeling of satisfaction.

_____

_____

_____

_____

_____

_____

_____

_____

_____

_____

_____

_____

"Fear can keep us up all night long, but
faith makes one fine pillow."

—Philip Gulley

CHAPTER 18

Inner Peace (Patience)

- The place of peace, the eye of the storm, calmness.
- Everything has its divine timing.
- When you stay calm in the midst of the chaos and drama, you will feel a peace that passes all understanding, a peace that doesn't even make sense.
- When you have peace on the inside, you bring peace to any situation, and peace will be what you experience.
- When you find yourself in the middle of negativity, chaos, or drama, don't let it in the middle of you. Shift your focus.
- If you get upset or bent out of shape every time things don't go your way, you can't bring peace to those situations.
- Peace is not the absence of trouble, getting rid of your enemies, overcoming all challenges, or paying off all your bills. When all of these things are happening on the outside, real peace is not allowing it on the inside.
- On the surface of the ocean, the waves can be thirty feet high, but thirty feet down there is a calmness. The depth is not affected by what is going on up on the surface. When we are living in peace, our emotional thermostat is not affected by the events on the surface because we are living from our spiritual depth instead of from the surface.
- Peace is about accepting what is (in the moment) and knowing that when we want to experience something different we just need to change our thoughts and focus on reflecting about what we want.

I am: _____

→ Where is it that you have the least inner peace or patience?

→ Does your lack of patience help or hinder your emotions or mood as well as the outcome of the situation?

→ Do the things or people you are impatient with have a tendency to work out when you are being patient?

→ Is there a benefit to being impatient? Are there certain times when this could be a benefit and when this could cause more internal or external conflict and less resolution?

_____

_____

_____

_____

_____

_____

_____

_____

_____

_____

_____

"Patience (peace) is an expression of faith that I have everything
I need. Faith, peace and patience are ever abundant within."

—Darlene Alisa

- If you get offended by what someone says or worried by every experience, you're not living from a place of peace; you're focused on the surface chaos and therefore living a shallow life.
- When you find yourself living on the surface and allowing your life to be dictated by whether the conditions are calm and sunny or windy, chaotic, and stressful then you'll feel lost and out of control. But when you recognize that you are on the surface and living a shallow life, then it is time to go deep into the ocean of your soul, your spirit, your calmness, where it is peaceful. Quiet the mind with meditation, or even take a nap.
- You can't control what others say and do, but you do have control over your emotional thermostat: your attitude, your response, and whether you stay on the surface or whether you go into the deep, where calmness, patience, and peace are plentiful. This is being in control of your emotional thermostat and not letting others adjust it for you.
- Put a sign on the door so you see it every day as you walk out or on the bathroom mirror. "Nothing is going to move me today without my consent. Go in Peace."
- Patience is knowing that even though you don't see a solution or have any idea how things will work out, you know there is something within you that already knows and will come through. This is when you connect with what you believe in, what you have faith in, and what brings you feelings of ease and joy. The answer may not come right away, but one always does. Ask the question, and an answer will always be provided if we are willing to be open to how it may come. Let go, quiet the mind, and walk in peace.

→ Practice this: "Internal and External Peace begin with the ability to step back, quiet the mind, and see everything and everyone clearly and without judgement (through the eyes of love)." —Darlene Alisa

→ Write down the area(s) of your life where you feel there is more chaos and frustration than peace, patience, and tranquility. Shift the thoughts you currently have about these areas to find at least one simple thought that is positive that you can start with in regard to whatever the condition or situation is.

_____

_____

_____

_____

_____

_____

_____

Write down the areas of your life or anything in general that brings you a sense of peace, and then spend more time giving those things your attention (instead of the ones above).

_____

_____

_____

_____

_____

_____

➔ Having patience and staying connected to your internal peace when life is overwhelming takes practice. The goal is recognizing what your triggers are and then learning to get out ahead of your impatience by changing your response before they set you off. You may need to take time to reconnect with the things that bring a sense of calm to your soul, that quiet the mind, and that bring the joy back.

• The tool in the next section (Have Fun/Play) is one very good way to bring about patience and peace when you are overwhelmed and stressed out.

• What I have noticed about myself is that the more I get frustrated and overwhelmed with how things are going to happen, the less patient I am. All of these things create an unenjoyable energy that is transferred to everyone around me and adds more chaos, frustration, and feelings of being overwhelmed that I continue to experience because nothing works out right. And the pattern continues until I do the thing that seems like the least likely thing to help—*play and have fun*! I distract myself from what appears to not be working out. When I do this, my energy changes, and then I notice things starting to work in my favor again.

• When we let go of the resistance, we realize peace and happiness were there all along.

• Peace doesn't mean to be in a place where there is no noise, trouble, or hard work. It means to be in the midst of those things and still be calm.

What are my triggers? What things get me riled up just about every time they happen? What do people say or do that appear to 'cause' me to feel frustrated and negative? (Nobody has the ability to change your mood except for you; this will become more apparent when you get out ahead of your triggers and practice separating yourself from your previously practiced emotional responses. The triggers will appear to fade away.)

_____

_____

_____

_____

_____

_____

_____

_____

_____

_____

_____

_____

_____

_____

"You cannot always control what goes on outside.
But you can control what goes on inside."

—Wayne Dyer

CHAPTER 19

Have Fun / Play

- When life gets too serious and the frustration, hopelessness, anger, agitation, fear, and depression begin to hamper your well-being, your success, your health, your peace, and your joy, then it is most definitely time to *play!*
- Reconnect with your inner child, your playful spirit.
- Having fun and playing is not irresponsible. In fact, it is a very important part of a balanced life.
- ➔ Laugh, be silly, goof off, dance, sing.
- When things get too heavy or weighed down in your day, view life through the eyes of a child. Immediately do something to lighten your mind and heart.
- ➔ Ride the grocery cart back to the car.
- ➔ Go to a park and swing.
- ➔ Color, paint, or go outside and use sidewalk chalk.
- ➔ Have lunch with friends.
- ➔ Get a scoop of ice cream (or something that takes you back to carefree days).
- Lighten your spirit and stressed mind, re-establish laughter.
- ➔ Watch a comedy or listen to a comedian or a reality show that disconnects you from your life for a moment.
- ➔ What other things do you find enjoyable?
- ➔ What are the activities that you like to do that allow you to feel good (that you may not do often enough)?

I am: _____

_____

_____

_____

_____

_____

_____

_____

_____

_____

_____

_____

_____

_____

_____

_____

_____

"In all of living, have much fun and laughter.
Life is to be enjoyed not just endured."
—Gordon B. Hinckley

CHAPTER 20

Acceptance

- Accept yourself first. Accept your strengths (without overbearing pride), and accept that which you desire to change (without judgment).
- Self talk: *I am happy with who I am, even though I'm not where I want to be. I love and accept myself as I am now, knowing that I am continuing to grow personally and spiritually.*
- Accept responsibility for your life and actions, and do not cast blame.
- Accept accountability. Our thoughts, perceptions, emotions, words, and actions create our life experiences.
➜ Accept things as they are in this moment, and let go of unproductive expectations. If there is something in your life you cannot accept and would like to change, then there is something within you that must shift first (i.e., your thoughts, perceptions, emotions, words, actions, and unconscious habits).
➜ Accept others for who they are. Do not try to change anyone, for this is their responsibility. We project onto others the way we feel about ourselves. The flaws you see in someone else may actually be what you need to work on first.
➜ If we cannot accept something or someone, we can shift our thought focus, self-talk, intentions, habits, and conversations to better-feeling topics; this will lend to a positive shift in our emotions. When we feel better emotionally, the things we previously could not accept become less evident and bothersome.

I am: _____

When you come across something or someone you have a hard time accepting, ask yourself, *How does this relate to me?* Do you need to gather more information about it for clarification? What is it that you cannot accept? Often there is something within us that needs to shift first in order for us to be more accepting of others. If you made a slight shift in the specific details you're focusing on, would that ease the situation? Could you be more general and lessen the specific details?

_____

_____

_____

_____

_____

_____

_____

_____

_____

_____

_____

_____

"Accept yourself right where you are, faults and
all. You're not a finished product."

—Joel Osteen

- It's OK that others think differently than us or have a different faith or do things in a different way. It is not up to us to make sure others do what we do, believe what we believe, or see life exactly as we do. Diversity allows for continued evolution in life.
- It is up to us to respect our differences and accept and embrace our individual natures while projecting a loving energy.
- When we are truly secure in our beliefs and who we are and are connected to our inner spirit, we realize it is not our job to change others. It becomes easier to accept others as they are, and we will not fear that they will impose their beliefs onto us because we are connected to our own convictions.
- → Accept that what is important to you may not be the same for someone else, that priorities and goals may be different. Habits, rituals, likes, dislikes, and the manner in which we choose to live day to day vary greatly. If you find it hard to accept someone as they are, then it is time to look inward and ask, *What do I need to tend to in my life first to better myself?*
- When you find yourself feeling let down, disappointed, or angry, ask yourself if you had an expectation that was not met. Release and let go of that expectation, return inward, and reconnect to your spirit. Accept the moment, embrace it, and move forward.

We tend to put conditions on accepting and loving ourselves. *When I lose weight, I'll be happy. When I make more money, I'll feel successful. When I'm in a relationship, I'll feel loved/worthy.* Change these sentences around. *When I choose to be happy, I'll accept myself and shed the weight I truly desire to let go. When I focus on the things I am passionate about, I'll make more money. When I accept myself as lovable and worthy, I'll come across the right partner who agrees with me and a relationship will develop.*

What do you have a hard time accepting when it relates to you and maybe even where you are at in life? Can you find a way to soften the way you are choosing to think about this? Give yourself some slack, and find a way to appreciate the current moment while you are shifting your focus to new and more positive thoughts about what you would like to experience.

_____

_____

_____

_____

_____

_____

_____

_____

_____

_____

_____

_____

_____

_____

_____

_____

"If you change the way you look at things, the things you look at change."
—Wayne Dyer

→ Accept that in order for change to come about, you must be that change.

• "Be the change you wish to see in the World." —Gandhi

• "A wise man, recognizing that the world is but an illusion, does not act as if it is real, so he escapes the suffering." —Buddha

→ Keep notes here about things that you know and do accept, things that lend to a good feeling within you, regardless of what anybody else thinks about it.

_____

_____

_____

_____

_____

_____

_____

_____

_____

_____

_____

_____

_____

_____

_____

_____

_____

_____

_____

_____

_____

_____

_____

_____

_____

_____

_____

_____

_____

_____

_____

_____

_____

"When I look back on my life, I see pain, mistakes
and heartache. When I look in the mirror, I see
strength, learned lessons and pride in myself"

—Unknown

CHAPTER 21

Listen

➔ Listen with your undivided attention and an open mind.

➔ Listen without focusing on what you'll say next. When someone begins a conversation with you, clear your mind. Be present in the moment and allow the conversation to flow where it will.

- If we respond too quickly when someone is talking, then we are not actively listening to what they may actually be trying to say and will most likely miss the point, setting up a situation for frustration.

- If we interrupt someone and begin to speak, it signals to the other person that we feel what we have to say is more important. It's frustrating, and what we have to say may not accurately reflect what the other person is talking about. This signals to the other person that we weren't really listening to them.

➔ When someone is talking to you, quiet your mind to be able to listen to them and ask them questions first about what they are talking about. Engage with them, or just be quiet and allow them to talk. Refrain from going right into your story about how you experienced the same thing and then continuing to shift the focus on yourself instead of the one who was talking first; this is referred to as *hijacking the conversation*.

- When we actively listen, we learn more about others and about ourselves as well.

I am: _____

Write down the new things that you learn about someone else or yourself by actively listening.

_____

_____

_____

_____

_____

_____

_____

_____

_____

_____

_____

_____

_____

_____

_____

"People don't always need/want advice. Sometimes all they really need is a hand to hold, an ear to listen, and a heart to understand them."

—Unknown

- Listen for the answers to your internal questions; this is your intuition. How many times have you asked for a sign or an answer but have been too busy, frustrated, angry, or spread thin to receive the answer? This goes along with **quieting the mind**. The answer will always be delivered, but it is up to us to be open to receiving it in any way or from anyone at any time.

  Be sure to let go of any expectation that the answer will come in a certain way or of expecting the answer to fit in a way that makes sense to you right away. This means that the answer to a question you have in your life may not make sense in the moment, but it could very well be the next step in a series of events that ultimately leads you to a full and complete understanding of a situation. This goes along with patience.

_____
_____
_____
_____
_____
_____
_____
_____
_____
_____
_____
_____
_____
_____
_____
_____
_____
_____
_____
_____
_____
_____

"Listen to understand, not to reply or give a solution,
simply to understand the person in front of you."

—Darlene Alisa

CHAPTER 22

Simplify

→ Let go of things, people, old ideas, and habits that don't serve in your personal growth or that may be holding you back from achieving your desires, your happiness, your dreams, and your full potential.

- Our belongings do not define who we are and do not make us happy. We try to fill a void by acquiring stuff, but it's a temporary fullness.

- We use about 20 percent of our stuff 80 percent of the time. So is the remaining 80 percent of our stuff contributing to our happiness or our frustration and cluttered minds?

- "We only need so much to survive, but this world we live in tells us we need more stuff to be happy. We're inundated with our televisions, the internet and advertising that says in order to be happy you have to have these things. When you say, 'Gimme, gimme, gimme,' you will always be in short supply." —Wayne Dyer

→ Simplify your way of thinking. If we think life is hard and frustrating, it is. If we think life is a blessing and joyful, it is. Our thoughts and perceptions create our reality.

- Simplifying is about all things tangible and intangible. As the years roll on, we carry more and more with us mentally, emotionally, and physically. These become dangerously heavy and can crush our spirits and move us further away from true health, happiness, and peace.

- Keep what truly gives you enjoyment, not just the illusion of it.

→ Which things or people are adding to your peace, and which are weighing you down? Let them go.

I am: _____

➔ Look in all areas of your life: you house, your surroundings, and so forth. What can be simplified, let go, cleared up, or completed?

➔ Areas to focus on are: work, friends, family, each room of your house, your mind, the thoughts you focus on. Look at the areas of your life that are frustrating. It may be easier to start with a small aspect first, like the fridge or the bathroom rather than starting with your closet, garage, marriage, or childhood.

_____

_____

_____

_____

_____

_____

_____

_____

_____

_____

_____

_____

_____

"When I let go of what I am, I become what I might be."

—Lao Tzu

CHAPTER 23

Daydream / Create a Vision / Manifest

- Daydream. Let your mind wander as you imagine what you would like to be, do, have, create, or experience in life.
- When you have become the one who is in control of your emotional thermostat by practicing the tools of *Zen Life Balance,* then this section of the book becomes really fun.
- → Open your mind to all possibilities. Don't limit yourself in any way when you dream. Let your mind wander as if you are a child again. Children never bother with *how* to make their dreams come true or if their dreams are *realistic*; they only focus on how it makes them *feel —happy!*
- "Logic will get you from point A to B. Imagination will take you everywhere." —Albert Einstein
- The easiest way to get what we want is from desire, not necessity. Desire comes from what we daydream about that feels good when we think about it happening or coming to fruition, not from what we want to get away from. Necessity is driven by fear, stress, and a sense of lack (e.g., the person or circumstance you want to get away from). We can't manifest our feel-good desires when we are stressed, fearful, and dissatisfied; those things paralyze us and block our imagination, as well as our connection to our true selves and, ultimately, our true desire—feeling good.

- → Your job is to decide what you would like to have or experience in life, small or large; it just has to be believable to you and create a feeling of contentment when you think of it.
- We manifest anything we want in life, as well as anything we don't want. Both are done in the same way. Whatever we put our attention and focus

on creates more energy that leads to the manifestation of exactly that. And more of that. And more of that. And more of that. Where have you been putting your focus in life? Which thoughts are you focusing on today?

- If you say "I want to be sick" or "I don't want to be sick," either way, the focus is on sickness. Instead say, "I see myself being healthy, whole, and complete." Now hold the feeling of that.
- If you say, "I am broke" or "I don't want to be broke," the focus is still on *broke*, and broke is definitely not a satisfying feeling.

→ Always focus on what you *want* and not on what you *don't* want.

→ Believe that anything is possible, and so it is. Talking and thinking negatively signals that you don't believe what you want is possible, and so it is. Let go of that subject for the moment.

- Faith is the accelerant on your dreams, healing, finances, love, and anything else you desire to have, be, do, or experience in life. Faith is living with the expectation that what you dream of is already in a state of manifestation.

- Manifesting anything small or large is possible at any moment. Perception of how easy it is to manifest something is always in your control. Change your perception to believe that nothing is too large to manifest because everything is at our fingertips. How and why you perceive life the way you do comes from your beliefs. Your beliefs are just thoughts you consistently give attention to, keeping them active. You can change your beliefs and focus of your thoughts at any time once you recognize they aren't serving you any longer.

Let go of worrying about the details of how it will happen, how long it will take, and what others will think. The only thing you need to keep your attention on is *what* it is you actually want or desire and *why* you want it. How will having it feel?

- The manifesting process can be delayed if you begin to have doubts about what you want or if you start to feel the need to control the process by trying to force it to happen.
- If you notice you are having doubts, it may be that something within you needs more clarification. It is important to notice this and not to force anything. Back off, and allow the process to unfold in front of you. Focus on things that feel good to you.
- The right people and circumstances will always show up at the right time if we don't interfere.
- If you feel frustrated at any time and notice that nothing you're doing is helping the current circumstances, then go back to practicing quieting the mind, releasing control, self introspection, and any other area of this workbook you may have gotten out of practice with.
- We don't *make* anything we desire manifest and come to fruition; we dream, create a vision, and align with our good-feeling thoughts and beliefs, and then *allow* it to come together, using our faith as the accelerant, while we are continuing to move forward in our day-to-day life with purpose.

What makes our faith effective? It happens when we acknowledge everything good in our lives and in ourselves, every day. This is being in alignment. How do we know if we're out of alignment? We measure and compare, judge, complain, explain ourselves to others, justify our actions and behaviors, feel defensive and guilty, and so forth.

- If your dream includes something that requires you to practice a skill, then it is most definitely up to you to practice and become very proficient in what you want to do (e.g., singing, dancing, public speaking, and so forth).
- Choosing a destination or goal in life points us in a particular direction. Choosing which path to follow (daily habits, lifestyle, attitude, core

beliefs, staying in alignment) is what will take us to our destination or get us lost and frustrated. You can choose the most direct path if you want to arrive quickly or take the scenic route with a few stops along the way. But keep in mind that if you know where you want to get to and you just stand still and hope for the best, you will not get anywhere. Decide what you desire, resonate with how that desire feels to you, and then take a small step forward. You will be guided from there.

- If you choose a destination or goal that is not authentic to you, you'll find that detours, traffic, roadblocks, and other obstacles may appear as a way to slow you down and allow you to decide if this is really what you want or if you're trying to do something to please someone else. This is not the time to give up. If you become frustrated, divert your attention to other things until you become clear about what you want. Go play!

- Avoid the things that keep you out of emotional alignment and away from your desires (e.g., judging, justifying, explaining, complaining, criticizing, rationalizing, comparing, and so on).

Every awkward, uncomfortable, and painful moment in life is always bringing more clarity to a desire within us. Instead of getting discouraged when these moments happen and allowing yourself to stay discouraged, angry, or even depressed, learn to get optimistic when these events arise. When you know what you don't want, you know what you do want even more clearly. Instead of focusing on an event that happened in the past, think about how that experience has made it very clear to you that you want to feel good. Think of a time when you experienced something that didn't feel good but helped bring clarity to a desire you had. Write down what you experience that creates undesirable feelings, and then from this, decide what you do want and write this down as well. (For example, experiencing particularly undesirable things in a past relationship helped bring more clarity to what I desire in my next relationship.)

_____

_____

_____

_____

_____

_____

_____

_____

_____

_____

_____

"Don't let fear keep you from your destiny."

—Joel Osteen

➔ Dream of what you would like to have, be, or experience. Create a vision—in your mind and on paper—of what this looks like and how it will feel to have or experience it. Next, you must find ways to connect to the things in your current life that cause you to embody the feelings and emotions of the very thing you desire, and you will be guided to the path of least resistance to experiencing your desires. For example, if you desire to have more money because you think it will create more freedom of choice and enjoyment, then your goal is to write down all the things in your life right now that provide you with enjoyment and ease. When you focus on and experience those things, you will attract other things that are also on the vibrational frequency of enjoyment and ease. That is the path.

What do I desire? Why? How will that cause me to feel? What are the things in my life that bring about those feelings now when I focus on them?

_____

_____

_____

_____

_____

_____

_____

_____

_____

_____

➔ "Begin noticing and being careful about keeping your imagination free of thoughts that you do not wish to materialize. Instead, initiate a practice of filling your mind with creative thoughts to overflow with ideas and wishes that you fully intend to manifest. Honor your imaginings regardless of others seeing them as crazy or impossible."

—Wayne Dyer

➔ The thoughts you choose to focus on should be ones that cause you to feel happy, joyful, and peaceful and that give you a sense of well being. When you find yourself in a bad mood, check in with the thoughts you're focusing on, and shift your thoughts to ones that uplift you. Watch a funny show or do something that lifts your spirits, or take time out to nap or meditate. Stay away from self-destructive activities.

_____

_____

_____

_____

_____

_____

_____

_____

"Freedom means you are unobstructed in living your life
as you choose. Anything less is a form of slavery."

—Wayne Dyer

"Give yourself permission to achieve your dreams."

—Joel Osteen

The Steps:

1. What do you desire? What do you want to be, do, have, create, or experience? How do you want to feel mentally, emotionally, and physically? Tap into your imagination, and let it run wild. Often, knowing or experiencing what you don't want helps you to create a clearer picture of what you do want. This step applies to every part of your life: relationships, health, income, work, family, and so forth.

2. Is this believable to you? It doesn't matter what anybody else thinks may be possible or not. It's all up to you. The only thing that matters is that you believe it's possible.

3. Know that as soon as you know what you want, your inner being and the universe are helping to lead you to connect with your desires. If you are mindful of your thoughts, emotions, words, and actions, the path of least resistance to your desire will unfold.

4. Being mindful is about being present in the moment, not missing all the amazing things that are going on right now. It's also about paying attention to your thoughts and emotions. Positive emotions mean you are focusing on thoughts and things that feel good when you focus on them. This will lead you down the path to your desires one step at a time. Negative emotions will lead you away from your desires and into more frustrations. When you are mindful of and care about how you feel, you can then know which thoughts and things you've been focusing your attention on and can make a shift if necessary.

→ The key to manifesting what you want and not what you *don't* want is in the consistency of being mindful of the thoughts you're focusing on by paying attention to how you feel. Adjust your thought focus to more pleasant things as soon as you realize you're out of alignment (i.e., judging, criticizing, complaining, feeling guilty and defensive, justifying your actions, explaining yourself, comparing, and so on).

→ Use the next two pages to answer the questions in the steps on the previous page and to make notes of what things help you focus your thoughts in a way that makes you feel better.

_____

_____

_____

_____

_____

_____

_____

_____

_____

_____

_____

_____

_____

_____

_____

_____

_____

_____

_____

_____

_____

_____

_____

_____

_____

_____

_____

_____

_____

_____

_____

"Believe in what you want so much that it
has no choice but to materialize."

—Karen Salmansohn

"You must reach the place where nothing in all of the
universe matters to you than the way you feel."

—Abraham Hicks

You Chose, You Choose

You chose to give away your love.

You chose to have a broken heart.

You chose to give up.

You chose:

to hang on,

to react,

to feel to insecure,

to feel anger,

to fight back,

to have hope,

to be naïve,

to ignore your intuition,

to ignore your advice,

to look the other way,

to not listen,

to be stuck in the past.

You chose:

your perspective,

to blame,

to be right,

your pride,

your games,

your ego,

your paranoia,

to compete,

your enemies,

your consequences.

You are not alone.

You are free to choose:

to let go,

dignity,

to forgive yourself,

to forgive others,

to see your value,

to see the possibilities, the beauty in everything and everyone - infinite happiness.

Choose to continue your personal expansion with intentional thoughts and emotions to match.

Choose to be the best version of yourself.

Choose to *be happy*!

Namaste (the Divine in me sees the Divine in you)

30 Days of Conscious Connection

The next 30 days are about creating a new habit of paying attention to the thoughts you'd like to focus on and the ones you want to let go of, starting as soon as you wake up in the morning and continuing throughout the day. The goal is to develop a consistency of practicing the *Zen Life Balance* tools by starting your day with an intentional, mindful focus and to get better at carrying that focus longer through the day. Creating this new daily habit of thought focus will allow you to be able to more easily tune into the things that help keep you in an elevated emotional state of being, even when the situation isn't most desirable.

You will be setting the stage for how you want to feel and will begin to recognize sooner when your emotions are shifting away from that feeling. This will give you the ability to pay attention to which thoughts you're focused on at any given moment and make a shift instead of feeling like others are controlling how you feel. You'll begin to empower yourself to be able to navigate through your day with ease and clarity, knowing that whatever happens, you have the ability to decide how you want to feel by being in control of your emotional thermostat. The beauty of all this is that your life will begin to present you with more people and situations that are a match to your chosen emotional thermostat setting. With consistent daily practice, your life will begin to evolve to new levels, and things you once only dreamed of will now show up in your current reality. It all begins with a desire and intention to feel better and a knowing that you are in control of just that.

Day 1:_____

Today's Focus/Zen Life Balance Tool:	Things/Thoughts that Feel Satisfying Today:
Positive Quote of the Day:	**(Self Introspection) Today I Learned …**

Day 2:_____

Today's Focus/Zen Life Balance Tool:	Things/Thoughts that Feel Satisfying Today:
Positive Quote of the Day:	**(Self Introspection) Today I Learned ...**

Day 3:_____

Today's Focus/Zen Life Balance Tool:	Things/Thoughts that Feel Satisfying Today:
Positive Quote of the Day:	**(Self Introspection) Today I Learned …**

Day 4:_____

Today's Focus/Zen Life Balance Tool:	**Things/Thoughts that Feel Satisfying Today:**
Positive Quote of the Day:	**(Self Introspection) Today I Learned …**

Day 5:_____

Today's Focus/Zen Life Balance Tool:	**Things/Thoughts that Feel Satisfying Today:**
Positive Quote of the Day:	**(Self Introspection) Today I Learned …**

Day 6:_____

Today's Focus/Zen Life Balance Tool:	Things/Thoughts that Feel Satisfying Today:
Positive Quote of the Day:	**(Self Introspection) Today I Learned …**

Day 7:_____

Today's Focus/Zen Life Balance Tool:	Things/Thoughts that Feel Satisfying Today:
Positive Quote of the Day:	**(Self Introspection) Today I Learned …**

Day 8:_____

Today's Focus/Zen Life Balance Tool:	Things/Thoughts that Feel Satisfying Today:
Positive Quote of the Day:	**(Self Introspection) Today I Learned …**

Day 9:_____

Today's Focus/Zen Life Balance Tool:	Things/Thoughts that Feel Satisfying Today:
Positive Quote of the Day:	(Self Introspection) Today I Learned ...

Day 10:_____

Today's Focus/Zen Life Balance Tool:	Things/Thoughts that Feel Satisfying Today:
Positive Quote of the Day:	**(Self Introspection) Today I Learned …**

Day 11:_____

Today's Focus/Zen Life Balance Tool:	**Things/Thoughts that Feel Satisfying Today:**
Positive Quote of the Day:	**(Self Introspection) Today I Learned …**

Day 12:_____

Today's Focus/Zen Life Balance Tool:	Things/Thoughts that Feel Satisfying Today:
Positive Quote of the Day:	**(Self Introspection) Today I Learned …**

Day 13:_____

Today's Focus/Zen Life Balance Tool:	Things/Thoughts that Feel Satisfying Today:
Positive Quote of the Day:	**(Self Introspection) Today I Learned …**

Day 14:_____

Today's Focus/Zen Life Balance Tool:	Things/Thoughts that Feel Satisfying Today:
Positive Quote of the Day:	**(Self Introspection) Today I Learned …**

Day 15:_____

Today's Focus/Zen Life Balance Tool:	Things/Thoughts that Feel Satisfying Today:
Positive Quote of the Day:	**(Self Introspection) Today I Learned …**

Day 16:_____

Today's Focus/Zen Life Balance Tool:	Things/Thoughts that Feel Satisfying Today:
Positive Quote of the Day:	**(Self Introspection) Today I Learned …**

Day 17:_____

Today's Focus/Zen Life Balance Tool:	Things/Thoughts that Feel Satisfying Today:
Positive Quote of the Day:	**(Self Introspection) Today I Learned …**

Day 18:_____

Today's Focus/Zen Life Balance Tool:	Things/Thoughts that Feel Satisfying Today:
Positive Quote of the Day:	**(Self Introspection) Today I Learned …**

Day 19:_____

Today's Focus/Zen Life Balance Tool:	Things/Thoughts that Feel Satisfying Today:
Positive Quote of the Day:	**(Self Introspection) Today I Learned …**

Day 20:_____

Today's Focus/Zen Life Balance Tool:	Things/Thoughts that Feel Satisfying Today:
Positive Quote of the Day:	(Self Introspection) Today I Learned ...

Day 21:_____

Today's Focus/Zen Life Balance Tool:	Things/Thoughts that Feel Satisfying Today:
Positive Quote of the Day:	**(Self Introspection) Today I Learned …**

Day 22:_____

Today's Focus/Zen Life Balance Tool:	Things/Thoughts that Feel Satisfying Today:
Positive Quote of the Day:	**(Self Introspection) Today I Learned …**

Day 23:_____

Today's Focus/Zen Life Balance Tool:	Things/Thoughts that Feel Satisfying Today:
Positive Quote of the Day:	**(Self Introspection) Today I Learned ...**

Day 24:_____

Today's Focus/Zen Life Balance Tool:	Things/Thoughts that Feel Satisfying Today:
Positive Quote of the Day:	(Self Introspection) Today I Learned ...

Day 25:_____

Today's Focus/Zen Life Balance Tool:	Things/Thoughts that Feel Satisfying Today:
Positive Quote of the Day:	**(Self Introspection) Today I Learned ...**

Day 26:_____

Today's Focus/Zen Life Balance Tool:	Things/Thoughts that Feel Satisfying Today:
Positive Quote of the Day:	**(Self Introspection) Today I Learned ...**

Day 27:_____

Today's Focus/Zen Life Balance Tool:	Things/Thoughts that Feel Satisfying Today:
Positive Quote of the Day:	**(Self Introspection) Today I Learned …**

Day 28:_____

Today's Focus/Zen Life Balance Tool:	Things/Thoughts that Feel Satisfying Today:
Positive Quote of the Day:	**(Self Introspection) Today I Learned ...**

Day 29:_____

Today's Focus/Zen Life Balance Tool:	**Things/Thoughts that Feel Satisfying Today:**
Positive Quote of the Day:	**(Self Introspection) Today I Learned …**

Day 30:_____

Today's Focus/Zen Life Balance Tool:	Things/Thoughts that Feel Satisfying Today:
Positive Quote of the Day:	**(Self Introspection) Today I Learned …**

Notes:

About the Author

In 1999 Darlene was diagnosed with leukemia at the age of 25 due to chronic mental, emotional and physical stress. She knew in that moment that she would help others in some capacity in her life. For over 20 years Darlene has been a healthy-lifestyle fitness coach working primarily with nutrition and exercise. She noticed that the clients who were better at managing stress had the best results, were happier in their lives, and felt more satisfied in general. Even though stress will always be part of life, she learned how to make small adjustments daily to positively affect how she feels. In 2008 she gave birth, 100% naturally, to a healthy baby girl after being able to be off the cancer drugs for two years prior to conceiving. In addition, she has become an Emotion Code Practitioner, in which she helps others release trapped emotional energy that can disrupt a variety of aspects relating to mental, emotional and physical well-being. Ultimately, Darlene enjoys inspiring others to feel the best they can and to never give up, regardless of the circumstances.

"I tried to please everyone around me and would strive for perfection when I was growing up, in hopes that their approval would cause me to feel good, but what happened is that I never felt good enough due to self-doubt and unrealistic expectations. I never developed the ability of self-approval. What I know now is that I must care about how I feel and that feeling good is my priority. And in this it has lifted a lot of the heaviness and brought about more internal peace." – Darlene Alisa

Printed in the United States
by Baker & Taylor Publisher Services